Walk in Power

Live in Prayer

Walk in Power

Live in Prayer

Six Principles to Make Your Prayers Powerful

by
BRIAN BRUNIUS

DRISHTI PRESS
New York City · 2014

Walk in Power, Live in Prayer copyright © 2014 by Brian Brunius.

All rights reserved. No part of this book may be used or reproduced in any manner whatsoever without written permission from the publisher except in the case of brief quotations embodied in critical articles and reviews.

Published by Drishti Press, New York, NY
For information: drishtipublishing@gmail.com

ISBN 978-0-692288-34-4

Library of Congress Control Number: 2014916796

First Edition

Dedicated to W.B.

*For compassion that brings me to tears.
Wisdom beyond my understanding.
And unrepayable kindness.
My eternal gratitude.*

Table of Contents

Getting Started 5

My First Prayer 15

Principle 1: Prayer Is Talking to God 25

Principle 2: Talk to Your Best Friend 35

Principle 3: Choose the Name You Like 43

Principle 4: What You Believe Is What You Get 49

Principle 5: God Only Has the Power You Give Him 59

Principle 6: Meditation Is Listening to God 71

A Few More Suggestions 79

About the Author 85

*To pray, lift your mind and heart to God.
Give Him your every hope and fear.
Let Him lift these great weights from you.
And let your clouded vision clear.*

~Roger J. Smith

Getting Started

This book is a practical guide to getting started with prayer, told through my personal experiences and using guiding principles I learned from spiritual people much more advanced in prayer than am I. This book can be used by the absolute beginner to build a healthy foundation for a lifetime of prayer, or as a review for those experienced in prayer who are seeking to get more from their practice.

Prayer is an open-source tool for spiritual growth and development. As a tool, it is extremely powerful, and can bring about rapid relief from suffering, or rapid spiritual growth, but only if you know how to use it in clear and effective ways. It is not a religion, though it is a tool used by most religions. It's like doing a physical exercise. If you know how to do it well, you can get good results. If you don't do it well, not only may you get no benefit from your efforts, you might even hurt yourself.

This book is written with the goal of jump-starting your prayer life. For complete beginners in prayer, this is a step-by-step guide to getting started. For those who have been praying for years, the principles espoused in the following pages will serve as a refresher—points to reflect on to improve and clarify your practice of prayer.

You can read dozens of books about prayer and fail to make the slightest progress unless you actually start to pray. And until you take the first baby steps of building a prayer life, how can you expect your prayers to be powerful and effective? Prayer works. The experiences of advanced practitioners in every world religion attest to that. It will work for us, too, regardless of our spiritual or religious background.

Often the hardest task in beginning to pray is overcoming the intellectual and mental obstacles that prevent us from opening up to the One universal force that pervades every atom that exists. We get so caught up in giving that force a name and figuring out how to worship it, that we fail the simplest task of making contact and beginning a conversation. We let our beliefs, or those we've learned from others, limit the extent of that relationship, and prevent us from making progress.

So, please, read and re-read the simple concepts on the following pages. Each of the six principles that follow is later detailed in a full chapter. Each chapter is accompanied by a section entitled "Practical Prayer" in which I invite you to join me in a series of prayers designed to open up and accelerate your journey in prayer. I promise these tools will change your spiritual life if you apply them in the manner they are herein presented.

Let's get started.

Principle 1

Getting started with prayer is a lot like sitting down on a park bench and trying to strike up a conversation with a stranger. At first all you have to talk about is the weather. After a few minutes you make a comment about someone walking by. Eventually you make a joke about politicians messing up the economy. And finally you say something personal about your life. That's when the conversation really starts. Because until the other person knows something about you and what you care about, they don't really have anything to go on. And it's the same with God. You have to start talking and spill the beans about your fears, your worries, your dreams, and aspirations.

Prayer Is Talking to God.

Principle 2

In simple terms, praying should be like picking up the phone and calling a good friend. You should be free to talk, say whatever you need to get off your chest, and feel like the person on the other end of the line is paying attention to you, cares about you, and wants you to be happy. So when praying, be sure to do the following:

Talk to God Like You'd Talk to Your Best Friend.

Principle 3

What do I mean when I write the word "God?" When I pray, my prayers have to be directed to someone or something. That force or energy I pray to, I call "God," because it's a very simple and easy word. I'm not thinking about the specific deity of any particular religion. I've come to believe in my own concept of God, and I use that when I pray. You'll need to come up with your own definition—one that works for you, inspires you, humbles you, and helps you to connect and feel you will be heard.

God Has Many Names and Forms. Choose the One You Like.

Principle 4

While you're busy trying to identify a name for the God to whom you will pray, be sure to review your beliefs about God. Many people have negative beliefs about God based on things they were told as children, or experiences they've had throughout life. For example, some were taught to believe God is punishing or vindictive. When they pray to a God of this nature, they will probably not experience feelings of comfort and security. Instead they will likely feel they are being punished—or will be soon—whether they've tried their best or not. Others believe in a God that is always sending them miracles and helping them at every opportunity. Those people are much more likely to experience miracles and feel grateful and cared for. So be sure to review your beliefs about your personal conception of God, because:

What You Believe Is What You Get From God.

Principle 5

Some people believe in a God that is far away, uninterested in interceding in their lives, or simply not powerful enough or near enough to help them. In this case, they either will not turn to that God for help, or, if they do, they will feel disappointed when there's no sign that God has changed anything about the problems they are experiencing. Is it any surprise?

God Only Has the Power You Give Him to Help You.

Principle 6

Finally, humans are cry babies. Once a regular habit of prayer has begun, we tend to run to God dozens of times a day pleading for God to fix a certain problem, send more money, provide a better job, make our home lives better, find us a parking space. The list is endless. Personally, I believe in a God who hears all those prayers and works to help us. I also believe my God is constantly sending me messages, signs, and opportunities to work through my problems. But often I am so busy pleading for help I forget to listen. So I've had to learn to take a few moments each day to listen to God, to be silent after I've prayed, and invite God to respond. Some people call this a form of meditation.

Meditation Is Listening to God.

*May all beings everywhere plagued
with sufferings of body and mind
quickly be freed from their illnesses.
May those frightened cease to be afraid,
and may those bound be free.
May the powerless find power,
and may people think
of befriending one another.
May those who find themselves in trackless,
fearful wilderness—
the children, the aged, the unprotected—
be guarded by beneficent celestials,
and may they swiftly attain Buddhahood.*

~ The Bodhicaryavatara
by Shantideva

My First Prayer

In the spirit of honesty and credibility, I'm not going to tell you anything about prayer unless it comes from my personal experience. So, I thought I'd start by telling you about my first prayer, and the miraculous results that followed it.

In 1993, I was a very ill person. I had suffered extensive liver and kidney damage, and was visiting the hospital frequently for dialysis and other medical interventions. I was angry and bitter towards most people. I felt no one liked me. I didn't really like myself very much. And I certainly did not like the idea of God. I believed that God was a made-up idea, probably for the purpose of subduing and controlling the masses. I thought if there was a God, He must be extremely cruel and callus to allow such incredible suffering to pervade the world.

At some point during my treatment, my health took a turn for the worse. The doctors began to talk to me about making plans for my death. My family lived in a nearby state, and I refused to allow the doctors to contact them. In a few short months, I went from a normal 23 year old, to a dying old man. My skin was greenish-yellow, my tongue was black, and there were no whites in my eyes. I smelled terrible, I was losing my hair, and I was consumed with hatred for everyone and everything in the world.

A good friend came to visit me at home on my sickbed, and he brought with him someone I had never met before. This stranger exuded peace and kindness. A few words from him soothed the anger and rage of injustice that was boiling inside of me. He spoke to me for hours, about what I'm not even sure. All I remember are his final words as he left the room that day. He looked up at the clock and said to me, "Look, it's 11:11. That's an angel number. It means something very special is going to happen for you." And then he leaned in close to me and said something I've never forgotten, "One day, perhaps very, very soon," he said, "you will be desperate enough to reach out for help. And I want you to know when the time comes that there is a kind and a loving and a benevolent force in the universe. It doesn't matter what name you call it. When you reach out to it and ask for help, it will reach back and help you." And with that he said goodbye and left my room.

I remained in stunned silence for some time. Recollecting how calm and peaceful that man made me feel, and his parting words, I tried intellectually to reconcile his statements with my own beliefs about God. But it became clear that my intellect was of no use whatsoever in this matter. Eventually I went to the hospital for my dialysis, and was checked in because my numbers were particularly bad that day. After settling into my hospital room late in the evening, I fell asleep.

Early in the morning, I woke up from my sleep freezing cold. It was the coldest I ever remember feeling in my entire life. I looked up at the digital clock on the wall and saw the time, 4:44, and thought to myself, "Another angel number. What does it mean?" But I pushed that thought aside as I felt myself shiver again. I reached for the covers to pull them over my torso, and found that I couldn't move my arms. I tried to reach for the buzzer to call for help, and couldn't even move the wrist and fingers of the hand closest to the call button. At first I thought it was because I was so cold, but I knew it wasn't cold enough in the hospital for me to be frozen immobile.

I decided I had to use all my strength to throw myself out of the bed and crawl for help on the floor. So I summoned up every bit of struggle left in me and... Nothing. I couldn't move. Waves of panic and desperation flashed though my mind, and then I became aware of something else. My view shifted, and I suddenly realized that everything I had been seeing was from a view above my body. I questioned how it was possible that I could be looking down from above at my body. I was captivated by the look on my face. It was so still and peaceful. And that stillness engulfed me. I suddenly felt a peace I had never known, and the thought flashed though my mind, "You're dying. This is what death feels like."

As I floated there looking down at my lifeless body, thoughts of the people I had known in my life started to drift peacefully in front of me. And then it changed. Those thoughts turned dark, and I had the experience of my life flashing chronologically before my eyes. Except all the people and events I saw were bad ones. I remembered every moment I regretted, every mistake I had made, everyone who had ever hurt me. There were no good thoughts or memories in this life review.

Somewhere in the middle of it, my view shifted again, and I saw myself in an industrial setting, in the middle of concrete-lined canal of blood, and all the people I knew were standing on the edges of the canal hurling insults at me, shaming me, telling me how bad I had been. As I struggled to stay afloat in the roiling bloody currents, the gathered crowd threw boulders at me, trying to drown me. My suffering was terrible, and the insults and barrage of objects seemed endless. My whole life had been a waste and I would die ignominiously.

Somewhere in the periphery of my mind, I could remember the man who had visited me the day before. I heard his voice again, and remembered his message that there is "a kind and a loving and a benevolent force" in the universe, and that if I asked it for help, it would help me. These ideas conflicted with my own long-held beliefs. I thought there was no God. And if there was, He was cruel, punishing, and didn't want anything good for me. I had been told many times I was a sinner and God would send me to hell.

But this man had left me with an incredible peace, and the seeds of a fresh, new philosophy, the result of which was a redefinition of my beliefs about God. And so, relying upon the faith and beliefs of someone obviously happier and more connected to God than I was, I prayed for the first time in my life. From the river of blood in which I was drowning in my vision, I lifted up my eyes and spoke to the heavens, "God, I know you're not really there, but if you can hear me, I need help, and I'm willing to do whatever it takes."

It was the simplest prayer, and, as it turned out, extremely vital to saving my life and beginning a new life in the spirit. In the vision, looking up toward heaven, I saw a blue light shining through the clouds. And that neon blue light grew brighter and closer, until it descended blindingly above my head. As the light touched the top of my head, a voice resounded in my ears and all around me, saying, "I am the blue angel, and I have been sent to take you to God."

At the same moment, I experienced a rising feeling, and the blue light held me fast, lifting me upwards, away from the scene of torment and torture playing out below. With relief, I saw my past and all the people I had known fade away, smaller and smaller, until I couldn't see them anymore, and after a bit even the memory of them faded from my mind. Nothing existed except me and the blue light, and the possibility of meeting God.

But the upward journey was not fast. We rose skyward for what felt like hours, even days, and as we ascended further, our progress was slower and slower. Finally the angel told me to prepare to enter heaven, and to hold tightly to its light. I squeezed with all my strength to hold onto him, and we popped though some invisible barrier, away from the blue sky we had been in, into a new place of pure white light, silence, and peace.

"This is heaven," I thought to myself. It matched the images I had seen in movies. Not exactly in the clouds, but certainly all white, vast, silent, and seemingly endless. The blue angel who had carried me there was now gone, but I was not scared. There was the feeling of a magnet pulling me, and a silent knowing that if I followed that pull I would reach God.

In my mind, I was imagining God as a human man about my size. I was thinking of all the things I wanted to tell Him, about how unfair my life had been, how fraught with difficulties, how much I deserved to succeed, and how everyone failed to recognize my importance. As these thoughts passed through my mind, I traveled through heaven until without warning I slammed into an invisible wall, and could move no more.

Looking up, I saw something big and glowing white in front of me, but since all of heaven appeared white to me, it was initially hard to make out. I stepped back to get a better look, and back further still, until I started to discern the shape of a giant foot in front of me. I was no taller than the little toe of this huge foot. And my mind went blank with the realization that this was God. It was a giant body of light, so luminous and blinding I could not see above the foot.

Stunned into silence, all thoughts of my life left my mind, and all the words I intended to speak were gone. In an awestruck and humbled silence, I again felt myself rising. It was God lifting me up like a parent lifting a child, into His radiant and glowing arms. And then we touched off from the luminous white surface of heaven, rising upward together into space. I could see God now the same size as me, and whether I grew larger or he grew smaller, I cannot say. I was in humbled silence, neither thinking of myself, nor merging into the mind of God. Separate, but at the same time in a deeply quiet state of awareness with no thoughts of self.

At some point He began to speak to me. The messages were vast in scope and significance, yet, explained as if to a child, made perfect sense. He told me why I was born, and detailed the role of every person I'd had in my life. He told me why certain events had happened, and expounded on the defects in me that had caused me to react to those events in predictable ways.

We traveled together around the universe, around planets, out past the sun into an infinite expanse of emptiness. He explained the creation of the galaxy, and man's relationship to the whole of existence. This experience seemed to last for years or decades. I forgot about my body, about the earth, and about living.

And then God told me something I couldn't for many years comprehend. He said the spirit that had been in my body had finished its work on Earth and would not be coming back to the body. He explained that a new spirit would enter the body, and would take over. I was confused. Wasn't I the spirit in the body—the same spirit that was traveling around the universe with God? He did not explain or ally this confusion. He was silent, and I pondered his message.

Without warning we began to descend—a gentle and inescapable descent back into the universe I had known, back into the orbit of our sun, the Earth's atmosphere, and suddenly, once again, floating above the hospital bed looking down at my lifeless body, mouth hanging open, face made of clay, no longer even looking like anything that had ever been alive, certainly not looking like me.

And the voice of God was with me, saying, "Now you have to enter this body and do the work you are here to do." And I felt a slight sinking feeling and my form whooshed down from the ceiling back into the chest of that lifeless, cold body. As I entered the body, I heard the final fading words of God telling me, "Sit at home each day at noon and wait for me. I will come and speak to you."

The next thing I knew it was morning, and the doctor was pinching my arm, calling my name, and asking me excitedly, "What happened?" As I came to and my consciousness returned, I learned that I looked much healthier, and within two days was released from the hospital, with plenty of follow-up care scheduled for the coming months. My skin was pink again, my tongue almost so, and the whites of my eyes were white again, save for some tiny brown flecks which would never leave.

Not only was my physical form apparently healed, but I found suddenly that I was no longer the same person. All my tastes changed. My preferences about almost everything were different overnight. The things that had been most important to me were now trivial, and new ideas previously unimaginable were now paramount. Most significant among them was the belief in something greater than me.

Despite the clarity in my vision that I had met "God," in the days after leaving the hospital I could not bring myself to use that word. At first I thought of the presence I had experienced as the "Spirit of Love," because I had felt for the first time immense love radiating from that body of light. Days later I began to experiment with thinking of it as the "Spirit of the Universe," a presentiment to the rapidly growing consciousness within me of the vast expanse of creation. Many other names and ideas followed as I began to read and learn more about other peoples' spirituality and the words and names they used to describe their beliefs and experiences. It would be several years before I could bring myself to call that force I met with in heaven as "God."

I did sit on my sofa at noon the first day I was home, and, not knowing what if anything I needed to do to initiate the promised meeting, I began to recollect the experience of meeting God and having the secrets of the universe explained to me. Within a few minutes, lost in my memories, I saw a brilliant light through my closed eyelids, opening them just in time to see my living room wall turn into a curtain of almost blinding light, and the form of God, again in my own size, walked through the wall and asked me to come with Him. Together again, we traveled around the planet and through the galaxy, and God again told me many secrets, explained the working of all that exists, and explained my immense and irrevocable relationship to the vastness and fullness of creation.

Each day for about a month, I enjoyed these travels with God.

They sustained me and nourished me for the next twenty-four hours and gave me proof again each day that I was not insane. The pressure in my life as a result of the physical and psychic changes was intense. All my ideas and beliefs had to be challenged, rejected, and replaced with new beliefs consistent with the new "spiritual" experiences I was having. These beliefs were foreign to many of my friends at the time, who met my stories with incredulity, hostility, and often rejection. Some old friends quickly left my life, and new friends came in to teach me, guide me, or just humor me.

After about a month of these daily meetings with God, I forgot one day to sit down and wait for our scheduled session. And from that day onward the visions stopped, though the growing awareness within me continued, and the inexplicable experiences and synchronicities that were beyond human design continued. In just a few months, I became a vegetarian, ceased all drug and alcohol use, stopped smoking, moved to New York City, and underwent a complete metamorphosis such that I barely recognized myself. Looking back, I don't know how anyone could go through so much change without disintegrating, and yet through the grace of God I did.

My spiritual journey has continued up to the present—at the time of this writing more than twenty-one years since the events I described. It started the moment I asked God for help, holding the newly-acquired belief that help, when asked for, would be given, and that when it came it would be kind and loving.

And so it is from this gift of an experience that we come to you. For this book is about you and your spiritual beliefs and connection with God. The following pages will be focused on you. I will ask you to challenge many of your beliefs, to open up to new ideas, and to practice your spirituality in ways that may be foreign to you. Are you ready to dig deep?

Lord, make me an instrument of Your peace;
Where there is hatred, let me sow love;
Where there is injury, pardon;
Where there is error, truth;
Where there is doubt, faith;
Where there is despair, hope;
Where there is darkness, light;
And where there is sadness, joy.

O Divine Master, Grant that I may not so much seek
To be consoled as to console;
To be understood as to understand;
To be loved as to love.
For it is in giving that we receive;
It is in pardoning that we are pardoned;
And it is in dying that we are born to eternal life.

~Prayer of Saint Francis

Principle 1

—⚭—

Prayer Is Talking to God.

Though the idea of praying might seem daunting at first, prayer is the simple act of communicating with a power greater than ourselves and far beyond our comprehension. Although there are numerous religions, prayer in various forms is a practice shared by all of them. It's a practice in every world religion because, quite simply, it works. "What does it do?" you ask. Let me give you a brief explanation.

The human brain is powerful, but also very limited. Unlike all the other organs of the body, the brain is self-aware. In fact, it sees itself as the center of the universe. It believes it is "me." It says, "I feel this." Or, "I have so many problems." "This is mine and that is yours." is a common thought. The brain is always distinguishing itself from everyone and everything else around it. Most of us have witnessed the phase in a young child's development when the brain becomes self-aware and the child begins to separate him or herself from everyone else.

In addition to thoughts like, "This is mine and that's yours," the adult brain also learns to say, "These problems are mine," or "My boss wants to fire me! How will I pay the mortgage?" Fear governs this train of thought, and keeps the brain enslaved in a negative pattern of thinking that often causes us to make choices accordingly, trying to allay the fear. People go to jobs they hate every day for years, not even looking for other opportunities, out of fear that any instability could lead to disaster. Fear of what has not yet happened, and what may never happen, causes people to live for decades in misery and suffering.

The problems that the brain thinks it has today, or may someday have, become all-consuming because the more the brain thinks about them the more urgent and menacing they seem to become. In this self-perpetuating cycle of negative thinking and fear, we forget the simplest tool for feeling better. That is to get out of our own brains, and think about something or someone else.

If we're lucky, the phone will ring and, upon answering, we'll have a nice conversation with a friend who helps us laugh and forget about all the brain's supposed problems for a few minutes. Often this is enough to break that cycle of negative thinking for a few hours and help us feel better. Or we might get a call from someone who wants to tell us how horrible and miserable their lives are. If we're lucky, we'll feel sorry for them, and the empathy evoked within us will help us forget about our own supposed problems and feel gratitude for the good things and people in our lives.

In both cases, what happened is that someone or something interrupted the self-pity of the brain for a bit and broke it's obsessive focus on itself. Unfortunately, some of us, when we're down in the dumps and feeling bad, refuse to answer the phone, or open the door when someone rings the bell. Our brains want to deny any opportunity to help us feel better when what we most need is for someone or something to interrupt our mental pity party. We wallow in self-pity, and prevent anyone or anything from interfering. It's like looking in the mirror for a long time telling yourself how fat you look, how ugly you are, and that the clothes you're wearing look awful. It never helps things get better. It only makes us feel worse. Yet most of us are guilty of that kind of behavior at some point in our lives.

Prayer is an invaluable tool to break this pattern. When we pray—or talk to God or the Universe—we lift our minds from the selfish and self-centered place of mental confusion and fear caused by our brains, and elevate it to a higher level of consciousness that is beyond the ordinary reach of the brain. No matter how simple the prayer, the effect is often immediate if the prayer has been sincere. We sometimes call this type of prayer "heart-felt."

My first prayer was definitely heart-felt. It was a prayer made in a moment of desperation when I knew I was dying. In that prayer, I reached out to God and asked for help, and I expressed my willingness to do whatever it takes to receive God's help. That is to say, I told God I was willing to stop being locked up in my own brain listening to all its negative self-talk, to stop looking in the mirror criticizing myself. I was finally willing to open the doors and windows, let in the fresh air and sunlight God was always sending to me. I was willing to change, once and for all, and to let God run the show going forward. I wanted to live.

The results of that prayer were dramatic, to say the least. It is universally true for all types of sincere prayer that within a few moments of reaching out and connecting to God, people report feeling more calm. Their mental chatter diminishes, and a sense of peace pervades them. Often their thoughts turn more positive, and they are able to accomplish the next phase of their day without being held back by fear or negativity.

The results of one prayer—or a single conversation with God—are not usually long-lasting. If our negative thinking has severely crippled us and impeded our daily activities, the positive effects of a prayer may only last five or ten minutes before the negative thinking returns and the prayer needs to be repeated. But the long-term effects of prayer are cumulative. As we use prayer to build our relationship with the One to whom we pray, that relationship will get deeper, we will feel the Presence more strongly as time goes by, and the effects of prayer will become more dramatic and beneficial.

If prayer is so good and so effective, the question is, how to get started? And what prayer should you pray? Well, the world is full of prayers. But, remember, heart-felt prayers are the most likely to produce positive effects, so, if possible, let the prayer arise from within you, and let it speak of the specific problems you are facing in your life. The following is one of my favorite examples of a desperate and heart-felt prayer that produced life-changing results, both for the man who prayed it, and for many millions since then:

> *In despair, I had cried out, 'Now I am willing to do anything. If there is a God, will he show himself?' And he did. This was my first conscious contact, my first awakening. I asked from the heart, and I received.*
>
> ~ Bill W., A.A. Co-Founder
> *Language of the Heart*, 1960

My own story was very similar. When I prayed my desperate deathbed prayer, I reached out to a God I did not know and asked for help in my final moments of life. Through a miracle, I was spared death, and my entire life transformed. I was brought into conscious contact with God and I never thought the same way again.

Your circumstances may not be as desperate, but they probably feel that way sometimes. And those feelings of desperation and pain make for sincere, heart-felt prayer material. The wording of your initial prayers is entirely up to you. For many of us, our first prayers involved these simple requests:

- Asking God to save us from the current problem.
- Asking God to reveal Himself to us.
- Asking God to teach us how to communicate with Him.

What's significant about these three elements is that they express a willingness or permission for God to come into our lives and work with us. And they demonstrate an underlying belief that, no matter how bad we have been or how much we have messed up in life, God wants to, and will, come to us, be with us, and communicate with us. They also presuppose that God is waiting for us to reach out to Him, and cannot do much for us until we invite Him into our lives.

Before your next prayer, please read the following three affirmations out loud to yourself a few times. Can you agree on a basic level with each of these statements?:

- God is near enough to reach me.
- God wants to communicate with me.
- God is powerful enough to aid me.
- I am worthy of receiving God's help and love.
- If I ask sincerely, God will manifest in my life.

The amount of belief required of you is not huge. You just need the most basic willingness to suspend your disbelief. If necessary, rely on the experience of someone who has more experience than you. When I asked for help, I was rescued, and brought into the presence of God, who taught me how to communicate with him. Perhaps all you can believe is that God did this for someone else. If so, that's enough to get started with prayer. If God can do such an amazing thing for someone else, who are you to believe that God won't do it for you?

Practical Prayer

Getting back to your next prayer, it will be best if you go into a private space, if possible. Silence may be helpful, but once you have a bit of experience using the methods I am sharing with you, you'll find that you'll be able to pray anywhere and anytime. Some people, in private, like to drop to their knees to pray. Others fold their hands at their hearts into the prayer position. Whatever outer form your prayer takes is fine, as long as it works for you and evokes the right feeling for prayer, or demonstrates the heart-felt nature of your prayer.

When I pray, I prefer to close my eyes if the situation allows for that. Then I take a few deep, centering breaths to empty my mind and focus on the conversation I am about to start with God. As soon as I feel a bit calm and centered, I begin to silently express what is in my heart. Since this is only the first chapter of this book, and for some readers this may be their first prayer in a long time, or ever, we are going to keep it simple. Further reading will reveal many more concepts and tools to apply in your prayers.

Here are four examples of personal, first-time prayers offered by previous readers of this book:

1. Lord, help me to understand You.
   Guide me in learning to talk to You.
   Grant me an experience of Your presence.

2. Great Spirit, please hear me.
   I am reaching out for You. I am calling to You.
   Please show me You are there.

3. God, please listen to me and take pity on me.
   My mother is sick. Help her get better.
   Please comfort her and heal her sickness.
   Help both of us get closer to You.

4. I believe in the collective consciousness,
   The spirits of all beings and creatures.
   I am a part of One whole, not separate or alone.
   I pray to all that is good, give meaning to my life.
   Make me a better person and bring goodness to me.
   I dedicate myself to serving You and all beings.

Each of the previous examples accomplishes the primary objective of prayer, and that is to communicate with God. Just like meeting a stranger for the first time, we usually start our conversations with small talk. We chat about the weather, local events, passers-by on the street, maybe politics. We need a little time to build trust, confidence, and a feeling of safety. So too with your first prayer. After the first few meetings with God, you may feel ready to start opening up about the really painful stuff—mistakes you've made, people who have hurt you, your deep fear or shame, or the worst problems that are troubling you.

I'm not going to write any more about the first principle of prayer. God doesn't need a million words from any of us. He already knows everything. The first step is for you to start your personal conversation with the "Spirit of the Universe." Please, if you haven't yet, think about what you want to say to God in your first prayer. Write it down if you need to. But don't be lengthy. Between three and eight lines is usually a good length. Shorter prayers are sometimes the most effective, because they are often the most heart-felt and sincere. Silent, private prayers, too, are often very effective, because the mind doesn't get caught up with sounding good to other people who may be listening. If you can't think of your own prayer, use one of the examples in this volume, or find a classic prayer in another book or on the internet.

Please, stop reading now, put down this book, and close your eyes. Say your prayer. Nothing can happen until you start the conversation and invite God to listen to you.

When you're done, we'll continue.

Although the people living
across the ocean
surrounding us, I believe,
are all our brothers and sisters,
why are there constant troubles
in this world?
Why do winds and waves rise
in the ocean surrounding us?
I only earnestly wish that the wind will
soon puff away all the clouds which are
hanging over the tops of the mountains.

~A Shinto Prayer

Principle 2

—⚘—

Talk to God Like You'd Talk to Your Best Friend.

The relationship between us and God is of paramount importance if our prayers are to be effective. For example, if I call someone who doesn't like me very much and ask them for help, they will probably ignore my request. If I call someone who is very selfish and self-centered and ask them to pay attention to me, I'm probably going to be disappointed when they take over the call and start talking only about themselves. The same is true if I try to seek compassion from a cruel person, or kindness from an angry person.

In building my relationship with God, I try to see God as my best friend. Even if I can't hold that perspective perfectly sometimes, I try to talk to God the way I would talk to my best friend on the telephone. Here are some of the characteristics I see in God that make Him even closer to me than my best friend.

- God is never too busy to listen to me, even if I call in the middle of the night.
- God hears me from the heart, without judgement or anger, no matter what I say.
- God is ready at every moment to send help, if only I open up and ask for it.
- God has the power to take away my fears as I communicate them to Him.

- God will fill me with peace and gratitude if I open my heart and allow Him to.

My best friend is pretty good at these things, but not perfect. Sometimes I do feel a little judged, or a little guilty. Sometimes my best friend gets tired of hearing all my problems, and stops paying attention to me. Sometimes he's too worried about his own problems to have compassion for mine.

Not so with God. My best friend can't do any of the above things perfectly, but God can. So when I pray to God, I pray as if I'm talking to my best friend:

1. I greet Him.
2. I tell Him everything that has been happening with me.
3. I express my fears and doubts.
4. I express my hopes for how I want situations to work out.
5. I tell Him I'm grateful for Him, and that I love Him.
6. I say goodbye.

When the conversation is done, I feel so much better. My worries have decreased. My fears have diminished. And I feel a new sense of hope that I have the strength to go on and do the things I need to do in life, without being held back by my own mind's fears and worries. God can do all of this for me, if I simply talk to Him the way I talk to my best friend. Unfortunately, many of us have old ideas and beliefs about God that limit our abilities to communicate with Him.

Perhaps the most common statement I hear from those just getting started with prayer is this: "I don't want to bother Him." Or, "If there is a God, He doesn't want to hear from me." Now, If you pick up the phone to call someone who doesn't care about you, or who is bothered by your call, the last thing you'll want to do is open up about your problems or mistakes. This kind of incorrect thinking, I find, is most commonly an excuse created by the mind to avoid the exercise of prayer altogether. That tricky mind knows it only takes a moment of prayer to loosen it's powerful grip on your life, and it will say and do anything to stop that from happening.

Another incorrect belief about our relationship with God that I hear very often from spiritual aspirants is this: "If God were to know everything I have done wrong, He would punish me or reject me completely." This statement demonstrates two common errors. The first is that God doesn't know everything. The second is that God is going to judge us and punish us for our mistakes. Experience has proven to spiritual adepts for thousands of years that this is simply not true. God knows everything, sees everything, and is in every atom that exists. There is nothing that is not God, so God cannot be far away or unconcerned. God sees us as perfect, and wants to help us grow to love ourselves and other more fully. In communication—or prayer—with God, we can ask to be forgiven for our mistakes, to forgive others for their mistakes, and we can ask God to bring us back onto the right path. God has infinite mercy for us when we turn to Him and ask to be forgiven.

There are several other common incorrect beliefs about God that I'll cover in the next chapter. Before we move on, please re-read the following statements from the previous chapter. Ask yourself, "What needs to change in me to believe each of the following statements?"

- God is near enough to reach me.
- God wants to communicate with me.
- God is powerful enough to aid me.
- I am worthy of receiving God's help and love.
- If I ask sincerely, God will manifest in my life.

If you feel resistance to any of the above statements, ask yourself, "Am I intentionally trying to keep myself from being able to pray?" If so, please take a little time to write down on a piece of paper what exactly you're holding on to, and in what way it is stopping you from having an effective prayer life. Though it will probably feel uncomfortable, share what you have written with your partner, or a friend, or even a stranger, and see what kind of perspective they can give you. Sometimes just sharing these deeply-held secrets is enough to produce the necessary change in us.

Practical Prayer

Having thought about the obstacles we put between ourselves and God, let's try some more prayer, keeping in mind the principle that the relationship between us and God is like the relationship we have with our best friend. The goal of this prayer will be to share with God on a deeper level than we did previously. As in conversation with out best friend, we have to share deeply about our own lives if we are to have a deep and meaningful connection with God.

In the following prayer, we are going to confide in God our deepest fear, or a great secret we have kept from others. We may want to reach back into our lives to identify a moment of deep shame that continues to bother us at times today. Or we may have a burning regret about something we have done wrong, possibly from many years ago. Have you thought of it? Take some time if you need to. Whatever it is will come to your mind again and again until you finally acknowledge and accept that it is what most needs to be shared right now.

When you are ready, sit with this thought or memory for a few minutes. Remember it. Revisit the details of the event. Remember what you did, and what you and others said. Try not to go into a place of judgement. Lay it bare in your mind, stripping away the blame and excuses you have used for years to keep it a secret. Read the following sample prayer as an inspiration or to provide structure for your own prayer.

1. *God, you know already. But I have a secret I need to share with you.*
2. *This terrible thing that happened to me, or was done to me, or that I did.*
3. *I feel so ashamed of myself. I have never been able to tell anyone.*
4. *I have never been able to ask forgiveness, or to forgive the other person.*
5. *But I know you have the power to forgive all of us and to heal the past.*
6. *I ask you to reach into my mind and my heart and relieve me of this pain.*
7. *Heal me once and for all, so I never have to suffer this burden again.*
8. *Thank you for listening to me, and thank you in advance for helping me.*

Now think about your own situation. Imagine how to form your prayer. It doesn't have to sound good. Talking about painful things usually doesn't. What matters is that your prayer be sincere and heart-felt. So get to it. Find a quiet place, close your eyes, and make the connection to God. Pray your own prayer, exactly as if you were talking to your best friend, who loves you and cares about you and wants you to be healed perfectly and completely.

Good luck. We'll continue in the next chapter when you're ready.

Forgive me my sins, O Lord;
forgive me the sins of my youth
and the sins of mine age,
the sins of my soul and the sins of my body,
my secret and my whispering sins,
the sins I have done to please myself
and the sins I have done to please others.
Forgive those sins which I know,
and the sins which I know not;
forgive them, O Lord,
forgive them all of Thy great goodness.
Amen

~Rev. John Cosins

Principle 3

—ɯ—

**God Has Many Names and Forms.
Choose the One You Like.**

The world is full of religions. Gods and Goddesses abound in the thousands. Some religions have one God, others have many Gods. It's not my business or my concern what God you believe in, or whether you believe in God at all. It might surprise you to know that you don't even need to believe in "God" to pray. The only requirement for effective prayer seems to be a willingness to believe in something. Prayer, in and of itself, is a practice that produces powerful results.

As I wrote earlier, my first understanding of "God," following my near death experience, was of a collective consciousness, or a spirit of goodness pervading the world. Preceding my white-light experience, I would have been best described as an atheist—believing in no God—or at least agnostic—without knowledge—and yet my first prayer, and many that followed shortly after, were not only heard but produced powerful, life-changing results.

So what made it possible for a God I didn't even believe existed to hear my prayers and change my life? My fundamental perception of the universe changed the day a stranger came to my sickbed and told me there was "a kind and a loving and a benevolent force in the Universe," and that if I reached out to it and asked for help, it would reach back and help me. This is not something I ever believed in before. I always believed there was nothing in this universe beyond my mind. I was, in effect, the center of my own universe, and so my life reflected this very selfish, self-centered view, and was accompanied by the kinds of miseries and sufferings selfish people know so well. Somewhere in my mind, I think I secretly suspected that there was in fact a God, a cruel and punishing one who wanted to torture me and see me suffer.

Yet, when I was exposed to a new idea, about a kind, loving, and benevolent force, that idea reached the deep-suffering part of myself and gave me latitude enough to attempt a first prayer. Looking back today, that religiously-neutral word "force" conjures up for me a sense of mysticism, of possibility, of interconnectedness, and I believe it was those associations of the word "force" that gave me a new perspective and enough of a chink in the armor of my skepticism to try praying for help. And when I did finally pray, it was with that initially vague idea of a "force" that somehow wanted positive things for me. And that force, whoever or whatever it was, heard those prayers and responded with astonishing results, saving my life and restoring me to health.

Today I have no trouble at all using the word "God." For me it's a very neutral word. It's like calling a bird "Bird." I am not affiliated with any particular religious group, and I do not call my God by the names used by any religious organization. I just refer to God as "God." For the ease of conversation, I usually refer to God as "He" or "Him," because it's easy for me, and not because I think of God as a man. I do what is simple and clear for me.

Having worked with spiritual seekers to help them develop their own prayer lives, I have repeatedly noted that one condition must be present for the prayer relationship to work. The God to whom we pray must be universal—a force that transcends all human power and abilities. I have heard it said that you could make a chair your God, or a tree. Yet all it takes is an accident for the chair to break, or a chainsaw to cut down the tree. These are not very powerful or universal forces. As I wrote before, the "force," the "spirit of human kindness," even "Mother Nature," have been used by countless people as a beginning for their journey in prayer. These concepts of a "Universal" power are beyond human power, and are powerful enough to transcend accidents or random acts of destruction.

You may already know the name of your God. If so, you are off to a good start. But if you don't, take some time now to think about what resonates with you, remembering that your idea does not have to be solid or fixed or permanent. For the purposes of my first prayer, it was enough to know that there was something or someone, a "force" that was kind and wanted to help me. Are you willing to believe that there is a force out there, that is beyond all human power, and that wants to help you? Even if you aren't sure you really believe it, but only hope it is true, that may be enough to get started.

Practical Prayer

This chapter is not only about the name you call your personal God, or what you believe about that God. This chapter, in fact, is about your willingness to stop the intellectual struggle that has kept you from making progress in your spiritual journey, and to open up, allowing into your mind, heart, and life the healing power of that all-powerful Force, the One pervasive consciousness in all that exists.

If you're still with me in this journey, please now set aside all you have ever heard or thought about God, about whether there is or isn't a God, and resolve now to pray the following prayer of surrender with me. In the end, our beliefs are insignificant compared to the immense power of the One to whom we pray. When we truly surrender all our thoughts, fears, hopes, and obstacles, and allow that One power to enter us fully, we will be transformed. Our lives will be set upon a new course, with a new captain at the helm who has a bigger perspective than do we, and more skill to steer the ship in which we are journeying upon the ocean of existence.

I will use my own words in this prayer. There is nothing particularly special about my words, except the ideas they try to express which may be new to you, and which are designed to chart a new course in your prayer life. Feel free to modify the words to suit your own concept of the force I will refer to as "God." Or find another prayer from one of the many famous and saintly people who have left behind a vast repository of their prayers to inspire us in troubled times.

When you are ready to surrender, close your eyes. Center yourself for a moment, setting aside any other thoughts. And let's pray together:

> *God, all-powerful and universal,*
> *Dwelling within every atom,*
> *Within every cell of my body,*
> *Within every thought in my mind,*
> *Within every hope and fear in my heart,*
> *I surrender my will and my life to You.*
> *Please teach me to hear You.*
> *Use my body to work for You.*
> *Make me fit to serve You.*
> *I give You my everything.*

Sit quietly for a few moments after your prayer. If you wish, repeat it again one or several times. Listen to the silence of the universe. You may begin to feel a sense of warmth, especially on the top of your head or over your forehead or face. This warmth was one of my first physical signs that I was actually connecting to God, and that, through that connection, I was receiving "something" from God.

When you are ready, continue to the next chapter.

*My Lord, direct me to be appreciative
of the blessings You have bestowed
upon me and my parents,
and to do the righteous works that please You.
Admit me by Your mercy into the company
of Your righteous servants.*

~ *The Qur'an,* Al-Naml (27:19)

Principle 4

―⁂―

What You Believe Is What You Get From God

I've written in earlier chapters about the limiting beliefs I used to hold about God. Experience has identified several beliefs that are critical for our prayers to be effective and powerful—the most important of which, as I expressed previously, is that prayer only works if we are praying to a force greater than ourselves. Having found a name or a concept for the One to whom we will pray, it is now time to review the most common mistaken beliefs we are holding that block our progress in prayer.

Mistaken Belief #1 - A Judging God

Many people have negative beliefs about God based on things they were told as children or experiences they've had throughout life. I grew up hearing that God would stand in judgement, casting the sinners into hell and rewarding only a very few people. Even the saints, I read, had to undergo terrible suffering and torment in life, and spend all their time performing acts of penance for their sins, to gain the slightest chance of going to heaven. So it was clear to me from an early age that if there was a God, He was not someone I wanted anything to do with. God, according to what I heard, was going to judge me and then punish me. And honestly, I just didn't want to live in fear of judgement. Fortunately, I now know this belief to be the product of guilty people, and not true at all. God is all-knowing, but He doesn't judge.

Mistaken Belief #2 - A Punishing God

It follows that if God stands in judgement, He will also punish or reward. The people who espouse these beliefs must really love Christmas, because they have made God into a year-round Santa Claus. As the jingle goes, "He knows when you've been naughty. He knows when you've been nice. He knows when you've been bad or good. So be good for goodness sake." According to these people, God is always watching, prepared to reward us with wonderful gifts if we've been nice, and equally prepared to fill our stockings with lumps of coal if we've been naughty. It's time to grow up and let go of this mistaken, childish way of thinking. God does not punish us. We create our own suffering as a result of our mistakes in life. And sometimes life just hurts. We mustn't fall into the trap of thinking that the random uncomfortable events in our lives are the product of God punishing us. Life happens. Not every day feels good.

Mistaken Belief #3 - A False God

I was one of those people who, watching the news and hearing about all the disturbing events around the world, would say to myself or anyone else who would listen, "What kind of God would allow such terrible things to happen to innocent people?!" Clearly not one I wanted anything to do with. In the performances of Sunday morning televangelists I saw God used by unscrupulous people to build audiences and earn a lot of money. In the speeches of politicians I saw God used to manipulate public opinion. Among my churchgoing family members I experienced in many ways the false morality of those who claim religious authority to justify judging and belittling others, setting themselves and those who follow them as superior and "right." So I came to the conclusion that the whole concept of God was invented by powerful people to control and extort money from the masses. Today I know God is the "One Great Truth," but there are many false prophets in the world. I have learned to ignore all of those pretenders and focus on my direct, personal communication with God, which I nurture every day in prayer.

Mistaken Belief #4 - A Far Away God

Another mistaken belief people share with me often is that God is a little old man with a long white beard. He probably looks grandfatherly to them, but he's hard of hearing, losing his eyesight, and not really strong enough to do much of anything to help anyone. They wouldn't want to bother him, or ask anything of such an old and decrepit man. So they leave him alone to his old age. He's also very far away, they think, somewhere off in heaven, which they imagine is on the far edge of the Milky Way Galaxy. With the combination of great distance, poor eyesight, and bad hearing, they're sure that grandfather of a God doesn't know what's going on with them, doesn't hear their prayers, and has so many of His own aches and pains to worry about that He doesn't really care too much about their concerns.

Mistaken Belief #5 - I'm Not Good Enough

The final mistaken belief I hear so often from people who are trying to pray is that they are sure someone else can do it better than them. They often ask others to pray on their behalf because they're sure they're not going to do it well enough to communicate with God and get His attention. This mistaken belief arises from the human conception of time and space, which seeks to limit the presence of God, the power of God, and the knowledge of God. God is in every atom of your body, and the air you're breathing. He is intimately close to you. There's no need to find someone who can shout louder than you to communicate with God. He hears every whisper of your soul, knows every thought, and is constantly present. The key things to remember about God are that He's all-knowing, all-powerful, and ever-present.

The Result of My False Beliefs About God

Because of my many mistaken beliefs, had I overcome my feelings of unworthiness and chosen to pray, my prayers would have been directed to what I believed to be an impossibly far away, invented God, who only existed to make a handful of people rich and powerful and pacify the masses. That God would have responded to my prayers with judgement and punishment, probably casting me into eternal damnation. It's obvious these prayers would not have produced any good results. Because of these many mistaken ideas about God, I never bothered to pray.

Struggling against these beliefs for years, and burdened by their weight, my soul grew sick, and my life became heavy with many layers of judgement and shame. It was this soul-sickness that led to my physical sickness, and the ongoing mistaken beliefs that kept me from the One cure.

Luckily, on my deathbed, a stranger came to my bedside and offered me some new beliefs. This man glowed with an incredible peace and serenity. Every part of him exuded a sense of magic and possibility. He radiated positivity and humor and light. Within a few minutes of conversation, I felt a weight lift from me. My mind turned from impending death, and I was able to laugh again. By the time he was preparing to leave my room, I felt a renewed sense of hope. And just before leaving, he said the words that introduced me to a whole new set of ideas about God, and a whole new set of possibilities. He said, "One day, when you are desperate enough to reach out for help, I want you to know there is a kind and a loving and a benevolent force in the universe that will reach back and help you." In one or two sentences, he annulled all my old beliefs and doubts about God, and made it possible for me to pray the first prayer of my life.

The Result of New Beliefs
When I finally did pray, to that unknown "force" that the man had promised me was "kind and loving and benevolent," there was an immediate response. I had a white light experience, and awoke the next morning to find my health completely restored. Within two days I was home from the hospital, and within a month my body began to glow with a vigor it had not known for some years. All my tastes and preferences began to change. I stopped drinking and using drugs. I stopped smoking. I felt a strong desire not to eat meat and to avoid sugar. My preferences for friends began to change, and without trying, many of my old

friends who were not good influences began to disappear from my life, and were replaced by new, positive friends who also lived on a spiritual basis and who introduced me to many new ideas and different ways of looking at the world than I had known previously.

In addition to the daily visitations I was having from God in the month following my life-saving first prayer, about which I wrote in chapter one, I began to read many books about spirituality, including early writers on scientific prayer, such as Emmet Fox and his famous, *The Sermon on the Mount,* in which he artfully describes the relationship between man and God, and outlines a practice of "scientific prayer" that he promises will achieve positive results. Armed with this new information, I began to pray fervently, and slowly, day-by-day, I built a relationship with the God I was beginning to understand.

Because I started to believe in a God that was lovingly taking care of me, I felt secure and protected despite the unsettling changes my mind and my life were undergoing. Because my experience revealed a God that would perform miracles for me, I started to watch my life and the lives of those around me for miracles, and I started to see them with astonishing regularity. And because of the intimate, personal experiences I had with God both in my near-death experience, and daily for the first month that followed it, I began to believe that God was very close, very personal, and completely accessible to me the moment I reached out for him. Over time I would come to see that my God is in every atom, in every breath, within me, within you, and within everyone else. That God can never be far away. He is part of me.

So What Do You Believe?
This is a critical moment for you. Get some paper and a pen, and start making a list of what you believe about the God you are going to be praying to. List everything that comes to mind. On the following page is the list I would have written in 1993, before I was given new ideas about God:

I Believe God Is (1993)
- Cruel and judgmental
- Punishing and vindictive
- Far away and disinterested
- A tool for bad people
- Not real anyway

Now look at your own list. Do you see ideas about God on your list that may be limiting His ability to help you, to be close to you, to speak to you? Do you see barriers you are putting up that keep your prayer life from becoming powerful and effective?

Here's my list today, after twenty-one years of living with new ideas about God that completely changed my possibilities:

I Believe God Is (2014)
- Kind and loving and benevolent
- Intimately close and always ready to help me
- Waiting at every moment for me to reach out
- Always guiding and rescuing me
- The only thing that is truly real
- Within everyone and everything that exists

When you see something on your list that could be blocking your relationship with God, ask yourself, "Where did this come from? How does this serve me today?" We all have reasons for everything we believe. Some of our beliefs are inherited from our cultures, others from our families, some from our favorite elementary school teacher, and others from cultural or religious institutions. But the important thing to decide now is whether a belief we have always held is helping us today, with the problems and situations we have today. If the old belief is no longer working for you, I hope you will find the inner strength and determination to get rid of it. You don't have to tell anyone else. I promise.

Once you've reviewed and challenged your old, limiting beliefs about God, make a new list, and again ask yourself if anything on that list is holding you back, or limiting your relationship with God. If so, go through the process once again of reviewing and revising those beliefs. Once you can look at the list and sincerely feel nothing else on it is an impediment to growing your relationship with God, give yourself a pat on the back. Much of the hard work has been done, and now it's time to reap the rewards.

Practical Prayer

Having reviewed our limiting beliefs about God, let's use this opportunity to pray, keeping in mind all the new things we are going to try to believe. Of course none of us is perfect. At times negative beliefs creep in. Some days the prayer connection to God will feel strong, and other days we won't be able to feel it at all. This is just part of being human. We aren't perfect, and we never will be. But God is perfect, and is always listening, even when we don't feel we have made a connection.

The goal of this prayer is to express to God all of the new ideas we are going to try to believe about Him, and which we will use in the future as part of our regular approach to prayer. As always, the prayer that follows is merely a suggestion or an example. Please pray from your own heart, using your own words and your own beliefs about God that you have just clarified and solidified in the previous few pages. Sincere prayers that come from the heart always have a much more strongly-felt effect than prayers read from a page without feeling or connection.

Infinitely Powerful God, the One in all,
Immense Consciousness pervading all of space,
Boundless are Your love and compassion.

I feel Your energy in every breath,
I hear Your messages in every voice,
I sense Your presence constantly.

Lord, I ask You for miracles today and always.
I call on Your power to protect and guide me.
I ask to receive the endless flow of Your Love.

Repeat your prayer at least once, and preferably three or more times, turning inward and examining all your senses to identify whether your prayer has produced any feeling of connection. Do you feel heat anywhere? A welling-up of emotion? Do you feel calmer after the prayer, or more agitated? Sit silently for a few minutes after your prayer and be fully present with God and with yourself.

When you're ready, continue to the next chapter.

God, grant me the serenity
to accept the things I cannot change,
the courage to change the things I can,
and the wisdom to know the difference.

~The Serenity Prayer

Principle 5

—ɯ—

God Only Has the Power You Give Him to Help You.

At the end of the chapter on Principle 3 we said a prayer of surrender. It's not important if you used the exact prayer I wrote, or if you used your own or one you found. What's important is the act of surrendering—inviting that immense power of God into your life. So why am I writing again about this spiritual principle? In the previous chapter, I wrote that "What you believe is what you get from God." That principle covers your beliefs about God—beliefs that reside in your brain. And your brain, faced with the immensity and vastness of the God-principle, is terrified of its own annihilation. It is scared that in giving away its power to the inexplicable power of a consciousness much greater than its own, either it will lose control over your body, which the brain believes to be its own, or it will eventually cease to exist. And this ceasing to exist is, in fact, possible. It is described in various religions as Union with God, Liberation, Enlightenment, or Self-Realization. So the brain's fears are founded, at least from the perspective of potentially losing the ego with it's power to dominate our lives.

Therefore, we cannot entrust our relationship with God entirely to the brain which, when it's afraid of it's own loss of power and control, may take slight and imperceptible steps to sabotage that relationship. So whereas Principle 4 is about your beliefs, and consciously choosing to open up to new beliefs and letting go of old ones, Principle 5 is about the deepest yearning of the soul, which is an element far beyond the control of the brain—a sort of safety mechanism that gives us the motivation to keep moving, even when the brain wants to drop anchor and stop this unpredictable spiritual voyage.

For me, the yearning of the soul is deep and almost indescribable, an endless, eternal feeling. It often takes the form of what I call existential longing, a feeling that this terrible burden has always been here underneath everything else, and nothing can ever make it go away. Have you felt this before? You may have slightly different words to describe what you feel. For some it is a deep sense of shame, or a feeling of never being good enough. Others describe it as a hopelessness that they will ever be loved, or that they are not and cannot ever be good enough. Still others describe an endless feeling of restlessness, that they must DO something, go shopping, make something, research something, an endless need to fill an emptiness that they can neither see nor understand. Some try to fill this void with food, alcohol, drugs, sex, video games, watching TV mindlessly all day and night, or constantly listening to music.

As I wrote, for me the feeling is existential longing. I am always running from this feeling by trying to make my life look nice, by acquiring all the objects and people and accolades I think will make me happy and fill the emptiness. I buy into the marketing that tells me to eat right and go to the gym, because this will help me live longer and make every day of my life healthy and happy. I follow the nutrition fads that tell me to eat this, and take that supplement, because these are the things that are going to save me. I regularly get messages from friends urging me to try this or that spiritual practice, because these new fads or this new teacher will change my life and make everything better.

All of this activity, this desperate seeking and movement, is prodded by the brain out of it's fear that one day it will no longer exist. And that deep feeling of impending destruction is a tormenting reminder to the brain that no matter what it does, it will never be able to escape this underlying reality. When the brain cannot find an exit from these burdensome feelings, it calls itself depressed, and seeks medication to take away the feelings. Even spiritual practices can be used to run from or anesthetize that deep unhappiness that is underneath everything else. When something happens to return me to the awareness of suffering or existential longing, I think, "Oh no, how did I get back here? What do I need to do to set things right again?!" And I run to my prayers and meditations as a way to escape from the suffering and get back to a perpetual state of feeling "balanced" again.

For the purpose of getting started in prayer, and making progress with our efforts, we are going to use this deep desire to escape from our existential longing or suffering—whatever that feels like for you—to motivate us in our practice of prayer. Using this motivation to produce a positive result may not be the ultimate truth, but it does point the way there and help us progress as we grow toward a deeper understand of who we really are. It is this pain, suffering, shame, hopelessness—whatever it is for each of us—that drives us, so we might as well make good use of something that seems to be unavoidable.

The first thing we must do is to make a decision—a conscious choice—that we are going to see our God—whatever that is for each of us—as three simple things, which I also wrote about in the first principle:

- Omniscient (all-knowing)
- Omnipotent (all-powerful)
- Omnipresent (ever-present)

Having decided that God knows everything, has limitless power, and is always available to us, we have directed our minds to a new way of thinking about our source. But we have not yet taken these mind-based concepts about God to the level of personal belief and personal desire. I gave you the following personal beliefs to think about in an earlier chapter. Please review them again:

- God is near enough to reach me.
- God wants to communicate with me.
- God is powerful enough to aid me.
- I am worthy of receiving God's help and love.
- If I ask sincerely, God will manifest in my life.

I asked you previously to review these personal beliefs, and try to remove any obstacles you hold in your beliefs about yourself that would limit the power of God to come into your life and work with you. Several chapters have elapsed since you last read these ideas. What do you think now?

God is near enough to reach me
Are you willing to desire a close God, who is present when you call? Or does your intellect still want to hold on to the idea of a far away God who doesn't much care about you, as an excuse for you not to bother praying. I know within seconds of praying that I have made a connection with God. I feel a blissful heat around my head and a sense of peace descend around me or blossom from somewhere within my chest. But perhaps you would rather keep God at a distance so you don't have to be disappointed when the things you pray for don't seem to materialize.

God wants to communicate with me
Are you now willing to desire a God who wants to and is always trying to communicate with you? I know from experience that the warmth of God's presence is always around me, waiting to enter me through the top of my head within seconds of me opening up the connection and inviting Him in. But you may secretly harbor fears about having this kind of communion with God. Are you now willing to desire this deep, energetic connection with a power so immense that you can merge completely into it?

God is powerful enough to aid me
Are you now willing to desire a God who is powerful enough to

change anything and everything, to rearrange the whole universe to accomplish His work? This means inherently that things in you will also have to change, should you choose to open up to this immense power and fully, completely invite it into your life. Are you willing to be part of the everything that changes? In asking to be rescued from the sufferings created by the mind, we are really asking to receive God-consciousness, which is nothing less than the conscious awareness of the essence of God, which is in every molecule of us and everyone and everything else that exists. And this is so overwhelming that some people intellectually prefer to believe God is not powerful enough to help them, to avoid having to let go of the separation that exists in the mind, thinking instead, "I am here, and you are there, and God is somewhere else far away."

I am worthy of receiving God's help and love
Are you now willing to accept that you are worthy of receiving God's help and love, and that God is waiting at every moment to help you? It's common for spiritual seekers to believe they should restrain their egos and tell themselves they are not all that special. Saints, after all, are supposed to be humble. Big egos never enter the kingdom of heaven, right? And yet the kingdom of heaven is inside you. God in inherent in every cell of your body, and in the very air you breath. In fact, choosing to believe you are worthy of receiving God's love and help is just about the most humble any human being can ever be—because it is an acknowledgement that everything that exists is God. And if you are God, isn't it time to start merging back into the consciousness of God? Ego, on the other hand, is the desire to stay separate. It's time to let that go.

If I ask sincerely, God will manifest in my life
Finally, are you now willing to believe in a God who will respond immediately and manifest in your life when you communicate with Him? This one should be easy if you have agreed to the previous precepts. For when you know God is intimately close, when you let go of the need to be separate, when you accept that God is waiting at every moment for you to ask, then it is not a big step to

believe that when you ask, God will respond immediately by manifesting in your life. Yet some people who reach this stage put up roadblocks out of the final fear of disappearing, losing their own identities. Don't worry. This is a process, and as long as you are in a human body, the self-identity will always be there waiting for you. But God is also there waiting for you, so let's keep making progress with the tools of prayer.

I wrote a few pages ago that we are now going to use the deepest yearnings we have to help motivate us in prayer, even when the brain and intellectual thought fail us. Here's an example of what that looks like in practice.

Some years ago, out of the blue, a very close friend stopped speaking to me. Over a few months and after numerous attempts to reconnect with him, I realized that I was powerless. He simply did not want to be friends anymore, did not want to explain what had changed in his mind or his heart to precipitate that change, and didn't want to have anything to do with me. Of course, during this time I was praying for God to show me my mistake and correct the situation, but nothing changed.

At this point I could have decided God was bogus. After all, I prayed for help and it didn't come. I could have concluded that God was angry with me, or that God didn't have any power. But instead I turned to one of my spiritual mentors. I told him the whole situation, what I had tried to do, and how I had been praying for God to fix the situation. He advised me that my approach had been somewhat flawed, and he told me instead that the only problem was in my brain. After all, that friend and I are both made of God. Not being friends anymore—or being separated from each other—is only a matter of appearance. It is not reality. Instead, my mentor advised me, "Pray for him to be happy. Pray for him to have all the good and beautiful things in his life that you would want for yourself—to be loved, healthy, successful, financially stable, to have healthy children, and a rewarding family life."

I began this course of prayer. At first it was difficult. Each time I prayed, I could feel the hurt and bitterness deep in my stomach. But I resolved to pray for this former friend every single time I though about him, which in the beginning was many times a day. I faithfully carried out the instructions, thinking wrongly that through my prayers I was going to change him and get him back as a friend. Every time I thought of him, I prayed for his happiness and prosperity. And over the course of about a week, after hundreds of prayers, the desire for him to be truly happy began to manifest in my prayers. I started thinking beautiful thoughts about him, and the bitterness and hurt started to fade. Within ten days of praying in this manner, I found I thought of him much less frequently, and the fear inside of me started to dissipate. I no longer wondered what I had done wrong, but trusted that I had put this former friend in God's hands, and that God was taking care of everything. Immediately my personal life got better. My work went more smoothly. Money flooded in to my bank account. My home life became easy and comfortable, and I slept very deeply and restfully at night. Most importantly, I had a striking sense of peace that permeated every part of my life. And my mind was at ease, no longer having painful and resentful thoughts about the friend who had abandoned me without explanation.

In reporting back to my mentor the results of the technique he had taught me, and how my own life and mind and heart had changed as a result of the practice, he explained to me that my earlier prayers for God's help with the situation were simply asking God to be a salve on a wound. I was limiting God's power in my life to the role of taking away pain or dressing a minor burn. I was asking to get my friend back and have the rift between us healed, but that very thinking was dualistic—me, and him. My mentor explained that the approach he had given me was designed to completely eliminate those boundaries and separations, by allowing and inviting God to completely come in to the situation and the people involved, and use all of His limitless power to transform us and our lives on a deeper level. It wasn't about getting my friend back, or even about healing him and his life. I had issued an invitation to God to manifest His full power in my life and do what was right for me. I had surrendered my friend to God's hands, and that put God in the captain's chair, with my full surrender to steer my spiritual barque wherever He wanted to take it.

God is in all of us, and in the air we're breathing, yet the air between our bodies seems to separate us. Imagine molecules of water floating in an ocean, believing somehow that they are separate from all the other molecules of water. To any outside observer looking at the ocean, the molecules are all just one vast body of water, not at all separate, and each is completely indistinguishable from the others. In the case of humans, it is our brains and their dogged insistence on being separate individuals that give us the appearance of being different and separate from everyone else, and also cause us all the pain and misery that life sometimes seems to hold.

By praying for another person's success and happiness, I was truly inviting God to change and heal me. I was creating an opening for God to heal the painful rift I had formed mentally, that said this "other" hurt "me." When I prayed for blessings for the "other," God was able to heal "me" and soothe the drama created by my brain, which was the true source of all the suffering.

After a time, I realized that my brain would never have allowed me, in that situation, to pray for blessings for me. Because the blessings would have meant the very annihilation of the separate identity that allowed the brain to keep seeing "me" as separate from "other." My brain would have used all its tools to prevent this, by telling me I'm bad, that I had done something to cause this damage to our friendship. My brain would have told me I'm not worthy of God's help. Or that I should be ashamed to go to God and ask for help after making such a mess.

Fortunately, nature's backup plan kicked in. Pain and desperation are a gift from God, at times, to make us do things the brain would never sanction. In the case of my former friend, I was willing because of my pain at losing someone I loved, to ask God to be more than a pain-reliever, and instead to change me and the underlying conditions. In the case of my very first prayer, which I've already written a lot about, pain and desperation allowed my mind to surrender control when faced with it's own imminent death, and convinced it to reach out for help to a force beyond its conception.

For the purpose of this chapter, and the 5th Principle, that God only has the power you give Him to help you, we are going to take advantage of this backup plan or safety mechanism that kicks in when we reach those penultimate moments of pain, suffering, misery, and hopelessness. We *have* to take advantage of this loophole, because this is the only time we can act without the mind and its beliefs hampering us, and truly give God, however you conceive of your God, the omniscience, omnipotence, and omnipresence necessary to make big changes within us.

Practical Prayer

So when and how do we get started? Being human, we won't have to wait long. It happens often enough that someone steps on our toes, or says something that hurts us and burns deeply for days or even weeks. Every time we recall these hurts or slights, the burning starts again, and may even get worse. Sometimes the burning is an inner remorse. We believe we are the cause of the problems, and we think a long stream of horrible, self-torturing thoughts about how bad we are. In either case, whether we are busy blaming others or ourselves, we now have the right situation with which to practice this new principle of prayer.

I cannot tell you now exactly what your prayer will be in such a situation. The wording will depend entirely on the details of the situation and the people involved. But the example I have given of my prayers for my former friend should serve as a good template for most situations that involve resentment or frustration with another person. Here are the essential components of this deep and powerful prayer practice:

1. Say the prayer from the heart *every time* you think of the person or situation
2. Pray for the other person to have every good thing you would want for yourself.
3. Ask God to show you if there's anything you need to do to make amends to them.
4. Ask God to change you and make you the person He wants you to be.
5. Thank God from your heart for taking control and doing what's right.

So live your life now. Stay in touch with God every day. But when painful or troubling situations arise that will be a good starting point for your prayers, come to these pages again and read about this new kind of prayer. During times of trouble or disturbance, use this new method that surrenders all to God and allows Him to take complete control of you and the others involved. Employ these new tools to give Him the power to change everything, in whatever way is best, without being limited by your own desired outcome, your ego's need to win, or your fearful hope that all can go back to the way it used to be.

Our Father, who art in heaven,
hallowed be Thy Name,
Thy kingdom come,
Thy will be done,
on earth as it is in heaven.

Give us this day our daily bread.
And forgive us our trespasses,
as we forgive those
who trespass against us.

And lead us not into temptation,
but deliver us from evil.

For Thine is the kingdom,
and the power, and the glory,
for ever and ever. Amen.

~*The Bible,* Matthew (6:5)

Principle 6

—⚉—

Meditation Is Listening to God

Finally we come to the sixth principle of powerful prayer, that you cannot have a meaningful and effective conversation if you don't listen to the other person. If you only talk, and never listen, what you have is a diatribe. But the moment you fall silent, and begin to hear the words of your friend, you open yourself up to new ideas, new energy, new hope. And so it is when we pause our constant complaints and fears and demands for help, and open ourselves to hear the sweet message of silence and peace and new beginnings that come from God. Listening to God is the essential component of powerful prayer that so many people leave out of their prayer lives. Without it, there's no conversation, and we cut off the channel through which God can bathe us with His grace and blessings, inspire us with His messages, and give us new direction.

A big obstacle for many people to this practice of listening to God is that often religions and spiritual teachers call it "meditation," and that word sounds daunting and nearly impossible to the average person. Many of us have mistaken ideas about what meditation is. The word conjures to mind images of yogis or monks sitting cross-legged chanting mantras for hours a day. More daunting is the misconception that meditation is synonymous with thinking nothing for long stretches time. Westerners who have tried these postures know that after sitting cross-legged for more than a few minutes, all one can think about is how much their hips or legs or back ache. And forget about thinking nothing for a long time. As soon as one tries to think of nothing at all, the mind goes wild and can't stop thinking.

I'm here to tell you that you don't have to hurt your body or undergo excruciating mental torture to turn your prayer life into a true two-way conversation with God. It's simple:

After you have finished your prayers, say something like this to God: "Dear God, thank You for listening to me. I am going to stay in this spot silently for a few minutes, listening for any messages, new ideas, inspiration, or guidance You may have for me. Please continue to teach me to hear and understand You."

After saying this brief prayer, resolve that you will sit or stand still for two or three minutes. It doesn't matter if other thoughts go through your mind. The brain never stops thinking, and we don't try to force it to do something it was created to do naturally. We simply try to ignore the thoughts of the brain, and each time it draws us away from the silent listening, we bring our attention back to the space of silence, letting the brain wander off, farther and father away each time we practice. Let it go off on its own and keep thinking all it wants. You are going to sit still and listen to the silence, while the brain does what it wants to do. After a few attempts at this practice, you will begin to understand what I have written repeatedly, that you are not your brain. Your higher consciousness, sitting in silence, will be able to observe the chattering of the mind and see that it is a separate voice being created by the brain.

During this brief period of quiet, listen deeply. In the beginning, hearing silence for a few moments is enough. For most people, it takes time to begin to experience perceptible communication from God. But experienced meditators and spiritual masters assure us that the healing and inspirational flow of energy from God starts the moment we turn our consciousness to Him, and for as long as we can manage to sit in silence and receive the transmission. For this reason, staying in silence and listening attentively for two or three minutes after our prayers conclude is enough to make a good start at meditation.

At the conclusion of this brief period of meditation, say a prayer along these lines: "God, thank You for communing with me. As I go out into the world, please continue to guide me, work though me, and inspire me. Thank You."

Then open your eyes and go about your day, knowing you have received succor and nourishment, and renewed your connection to the One True Source of all that exists. You have been filled with new strength and energy to carry out the tasks ahead of you for the day.

The "voice of God" comes to some as a feeling in the body, perhaps heat or tingling. For others it comes as a very quiet whispering in their ear, or a complete idea or knowing that just pops into their heads. Others report that one or several images flash through their minds, which become meaningful as the day progresses. For me, I often hear myself conversing with someone else, and later in the day, when this exact conversation invariably happens, I know how I should respond to what would otherwise be a difficult or frustrating event. Many others neither hear nor see anything, but simply experience the silence deeply, and that silence becomes the main objective for their "listening" practice.

After this period of meditation, most people report feeling refreshed, more peaceful, and more quiet. They describe a sense of ease and gentleness. Since the entire practice of prayer and meditation can be accomplished in only a few minutes, it is easy enough to pause during tense or stressful moments, or before very serious conversations are to begin, and pray briefly to God, asking for the right words to come from our lips, and for the strength and courage to say what needs to be said, and then to pause for a minute and allow God to fill us with the help we have requested. Many feel the energy of God descending through the crown and forehead, sometimes as far down as the heart or solar plexus. After some practice, most people do begin to know the feeling that occurs in their bodies when they have established a strong connection to the Source.

Practical Prayer

Having now completed the circuit in which the flow of spiritual energy travels—from us to God in the form of prayer, and from God to us during the brief period of meditation—let us now pray together one last time for the purposes of the inner development this short book seeks to foster.

This longer prayer seeks to summarize all we have prayed in the previous five chapters, and incorporates just a few minutes of silent listening at its conclusion. As always, the exact wording is at your discretion. Here are the key elements to make your prayer powerful:

1. Help me to connect to You and receive Your messages.
2. Forgive my mistakes and help me forgive others.
3. I surrender my life to You and ask You to make me better.
4. I am ready and willing to give You complete power and control.
5. Use Your immense power to resolve the various problems I face.
6. I will be silent now and receive Your healing transmission.

Remember that brief, silent, heart-felt prayers are often the most powerful. So the prayer you use now should be directly personal and meaningful to you. And when you pray, it should be in a place where you will have a few minutes of privacy to have this deep and revealing conversation with God, and where you will have a few minutes of peace to sit quietly and listen, receiving the transmission of God's loving energy to you. Following is an example of a prayer that incorporates these six elements.

Personalize it as you wish, or write your own.

> *God, I open myself to You and Your immense power.*
> *I give You my worst shame and blame, my anger and frustration.*
> *I surrender myself completely to You and ask You to heal me.*
> *Please take control of my life and all the situations I face.*
> *You alone have the power to resolve everything for the best.*
> *In silence now I will sit to receive Your blessings, grace, and messages.*

(Sit in silence now for a few minutes. Then continue.)

> *Thank you, Lord, for Your immense love.*
> *Please be with me throughout the day.*
> *Work through me for the benefit of all.*
> *Guide me at each step, and show me a new way to live.*

Now continue your day. Should you begin to feel agitated or angry, confused or unsure, stop for a few minutes and repeat the prayer and meditation, again allowing God to come back into your life and take control. You will find as you repeat this process over several weeks that the periods of peace after each prayer get longer and longer.

Many beginners report that after three to six months of practicing this technique, they can go days or weeks without feeling much frustration or uncertainty. They start to feel the constant presence of their God, working through them and the situations in their lives. They feel the voice of God at times speak through them, or the immediate knowledge of what they need to say or do next enters their minds, and produces beneficial results for them and those around them.

I can promise you results will follow this practice, but only if you commit to it as a frequent exercise. This should be done at least once a day, and preferably repeated throughout the day each time you feel yourself getting off-center. God does have the power to restore your balance, but only if you open the connection through prayer, and then sit quietly in meditation to receive the flow of healing balm from the "Great Physician."

This idea of God as the true source of healing energy for our souls is found in many religions, and is beautifully expressed in spirituals sung by suffering people like us looking for relief from the pains of daily living. Here are the lyrics of one of my favorite songs that express this idea:

> *There is a balm in Gilead*
> *To make the wounded whole;*
> *There is a balm in Gilead*
> *To heal the sin-sick soul.*
>
> *Some times I feel discouraged,*
> *And think my work's in vain,*
> *But then the Holy Spirit*
> *Revives my soul again.*

Your prayers to God will be your own powerful song, expressing the yearning of your soul for wholeness and union with the Source.

Oh God! You are the Giver of Life,
Remover of pain and sorrow,
The Bestower of happiness,
Oh! Creator of the Universe,
May I receive Thy supreme sin-destroying light,
May You guide my intellect in the right direction.

~The Rigveda (3.62.10)

A Few More Suggestions

The previous six chapters have outlined principles of practical prayer which, if followed rigorously, will produce life-changing results. But prayer and meditation, after connecting us to the flow of healing power and the source of all wisdom, cannot solve all our problems. We have to participate in life, spreading the nurturing energy we have received from God, and applying the wise council we have received through our periods of meditation. Failing to participate in the world and allow God to work through us produces a spiritual short-circuit. "For as the body without the spirit is dead, so faith without works is dead also," according to the book of James in the Bible. We have to be out in the world, participating in life, providing the eyes and ears and hands and feet for God to use and work through.

Yet a significant part of being human is the desire to escape from feelings of pain, fear, and suffering. All of us at times live with the false idea that if we do everything exactly right, we will feel good and have no significant problems. Of course, the truth is that life has ups and downs, and often seems unfair. All of us have good days and bad days, good months and bad months. We may be lucky enough to go through protracted periods during which everything goes our way and we feel good most of the time, but this cannot last forever. Eventually circumstances change, and we face periods in which everything seems to turn against us and we feel like we'll never be happy again.

Following are some practical suggestions about approaches to living that will extend the benefits of your new found spiritual practices.

Gratitude

In the continuing cycles of positivity and negativity, use prayer to express your gratitude for all the good things around you, and for the positive aspects of your life. Gratitude as an emotion, and as a way of looking at the world, produces profound results, and seems to inspire God to continue working through us and blessing us. The difference between success and failure in spiritual life is often as simple as maintaining a state of gratitude, regardless of outside appearances and feelings. Any health care provider can share amazing stories about patients who, in the face of incredible suffering and impending death, have brightened all the people around them with their gratitude and warm-heartedness. And any banker can tell you about a client with many million of dollars in the bank, perfect health, and every reason in the world to be happy, who makes everyone around them miserable. Choose to express gratitude for waking up today, for having food to eat, for clean clothing, for having the leisure time to read a book like this. Most people in the world do not have the basic luxuries you are enjoying today, even when you are sitting around feeling miserable.

Surrender

Surrender is an important practice in your spiritual life. Instead of laying awake at night worrying about things that are beyond your ability to change right now, try praying, "OK God, this problem is beyond me right now. You take care of it. Let me know what, if anything, you need me to do to participate in solving this problem. But for now, I leave it completely in your hands. You worry about it." Not only will practicing this technique of surrender every single time you feel anxious or worried give you increased peace of mind, but the minute you let go of being in charge, you open the door for God to cast the light of His wisdom and power into the situation to reveal the meaning and message—often that a change in course is necessary and good, and that all you can do is hold on and wait for it to be done. If you make a habit of this practice, you'll find that huge problems seem to disappear almost overnight.

Do Your Part

We all know that as adults we have to use common sense, but when we're feeling depressed, angry, or shameful, we often go to great lengths to avoid common-sense solutions. So in this spiritual work, we often have to be reminded that the right actions to take with virtually all vexing problems are: 1. Ask God for help; 2. Tell at least one other person about the problem; 3. Do what you can; 4. Then surrender the situation into God's hands.

Make yourself a part of the solution to your problems. Don't just pray and expect God to take care of everything for you. If you are sick, go to the doctor. If you have a toothache, go to the dentist. If you need a job, go out and look for one. Ask God for the strength, courage, and support to fulfill your daily responsibilities, tell another person what is going on and what actions you propose to take, and then take the necessary actions with faith that God is helping you.

Banish Fear

If fear is an obstacle that is paralyzing you and preventing you from taking action, pray very strongly each time the fear arises for God to take it away and inspire you as to the next right action to take. And then do it. Don't wait until the inspiration has faded to take the action, or you will have squandered the energy transmission God has given to you to help you complete the task. Sometimes God leads us step-by-step. Take the action. Then when the fear arises again, repeat your prayer for the fear to be removed, asking for inspiration to take the next step, and then taking the indicated action. After you have done this a few times, you will find that the entire problem has worked out for the best, or disappeared without leaving any remaining challenges.

God's Will, Not Yours

One big mistake you make in prayer is assuming that if you pray right, you will get everything you want. Or you may assume that if you're not getting everything you want, exactly as you want it, that you must be doing something wrong. This is simply incorrect thinking. God's answer to your requests is sometimes going to be "No," usually because God has better plans for you that don't match your desires. When you don't get what you want, resist the urge to be childish and blame God, or, worse, turn away from Him. "I didn't get what I want. Therefore either God didn't listen to me, or this is proof that there is no God." Go back to your beliefs about God and review what you have written. Reaffirm that your God cares about you, and is arranging the world around you in the way that is best for you, even if, at times, it doesn't match your desires or feel or look particularly good.

Share With Others
The final and most important tip I can give you about developing your spiritual life in general and your prayer life specifically, is to share what you have learned with others, through your own story and experiences, if possible, just as I have done in telling you my story. God gives each of us our own experiences with Him and our own stories for a reason—they are imbued with immense spiritual power to help others learn to connect to God. When we share our stories, God beams His light and energy toward the listener, and fills them up with hope and inspiration. We are the conduits that help enable this flow of energy, simply by opening our mouths and allowing the stories to flow.

To the extent that you help others in any regard, and especially in the spiritual realm, surrendering the results to God, to that extent will God work through you, refine you, perfect you, and bless you. Each day in your prayers, ask God to give you opportunities and inspiration to help others. While some have followed this path to sainthood, for most the outcome will be an otherwise normal life filled with purpose, meaning, and fulfillment beyond what was previously experienced or hoped for.

I will close this book with the following prayer, which I use often. The words on the next page were suggested to me by a wise mentor many years ago. May they serve you as well as they have me to evoke the experience of God within yourself.

Lord,
See through my eyes.
Hear through my ears.
Speak through my lips.
Think through my brain.
Work through my hands.
Move through my feet.
Love through my heart.
Take all of me today.
Use me in the best way.
Make me fit to serve you.

~ Anonymous

About the Author

Photo: Joel Gordon

BRIAN BRUNIUS is a spiritual seeker who has found enough answers to begin to help and mentor others in their own spiritual journeys. He operates the NYC Reiki Center, where he practices and teaches Usui Shiki Ryoho, the hands-on Japanese art of Reiki energy healing and spiritual development. And he travels to teach Reiki classes and lecture on spiritual growth, Reiki, and other topics. He lives in New York City.

http://www.BrianBrunius.com

www.ingramcontent.com/pod-product-compliance
Lightning Source LLC
Chambersburg PA
CBHW060211050426
42446CB00013B/3050